CONTENTS

PAGE

Copyright © MCMLXXXI by arrangement with the British Broadcasting Corporation.
All rights reserved throughout the world.
Published in Great Britain by Stafford Pemberton Publishing Ltd.,
The Ruskin Chambers, Drury Lane, Knutsford, Cheshire WA16 6HA.
Printed and bound in Italy
0 86030 336 5

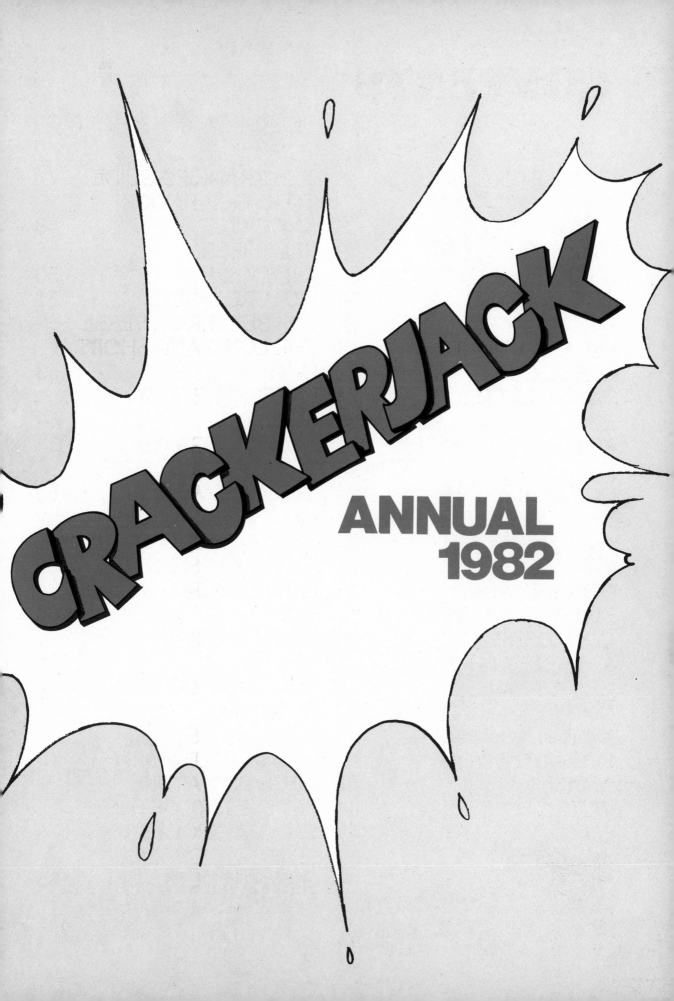

PROFILE ON STU

Stu Francis lists 'keeping fit' as one of his favourite pastimes, and fit is certainly something he needs to be with a career which keeps him as busy as his does.

In fact, there was a time when Stu hoped to take up sport as a full-time career. He, along with thousands of other schoolboys, had the ambition to become a professional footballer, but after a promising start as a member of his home town's youth team, his interests widened and a career in comedy became a promising proposition.

Despite the fact that he insists that he was not the class clown, Stu was making a mark for himself whilst still in his teens. He began his career in the holiday camps, like a lot of other famous entertainers, and it wasn't long before his unique brand of humour was in demand elsewhere. His popularity grew in clubs, the theatre and on television and in 1974 he was voted 'Comedian of the Year' by the show business newspaper, 'The Stage'.

But Stu's brand of humour isn't just admired in this country, he has travelled extensively abroad, especially to Canada, where he was a great hit.

1978, presented Stu with a great opportunity, the chance to star in a show called "Sit Thi Deawn" for the BBC—the first series was such a success that Stu was invited back for a second one. Between times, he appeared on 'Seaside Special" and "The Ronnie Corbett Show" and played a fantastic summer season with fellow comedian, Les Dawson.

Success followed success, another series for the BBC with Berni Flint, called "Berni and Stu", and a hugely successful pantomime, when Stu played the part of Billy Crusoe, Robinson Crusoe's brother!

After another very successful summer season in 1980, the BBC asked Stu to compere a new series of Crackerjack. The programme gained record viewing figures and people throughout the land could be heard muttering "I could crush a grape" and "I could rip a tissue"! Stu's success was assured.

And if you don't think all this keeps Stu busy enough, he also writes some of his own material, including some for the Crackerjack programmes and some for his other stage and club appearances.

Even at home, Stu Francis doesn't like to keep still, his favourite hobby is running! In fact, he likes all kinds of sports, both to play and watch. And it's at home that you'll find Stu's greatest fans—his family. He has two children, Andrew and Zoe, who are glued to the television, whenever Dad's on **CRACKERJACK!**

The Back-door Weatherman

If you're never sure whether to believe the weather forecast on the radio or not, why not make a weather indicator of your own.

You'll need:
A piece of thick card
Some thin wire
A large pine cone
A cocktail stick
Crayons

All you have to do:
Fasten the cone securely to the piece of card with the wire. Stick the cocktail stick under one of the pine cone's scales. At the top of the card crayon a symbol for sunny weather, half-way down do one for when the weather is overcast and at the bottom draw a symbol for rainy weather. hang it outside and see what happens. In fine weather the scales on the cone open up, allowing the cocktail stick to point upwards. If the weather is overcast, the scales will stay partially closed and if the weather is wet, the scales will stay closed, pointing the cocktail stick down towards the rainy weather symbol. Nature's way of helping you!

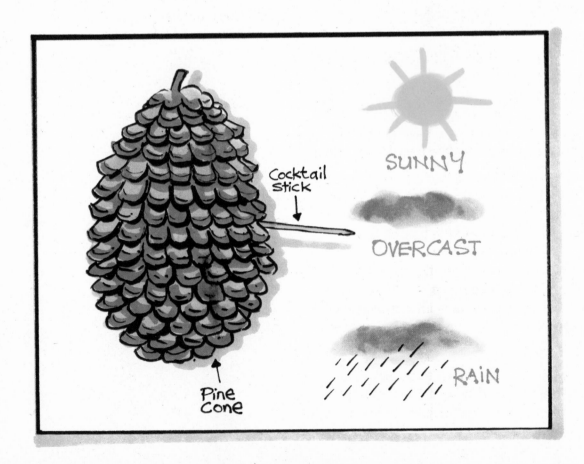

Cocktail Stick

SUNNY

OVERCAST

RAIN

Pine Cone

I DON'T BELIEVE IT!

In the thirteenth century, the Tartars had a princess called Shining Moon, who was renowned throughout the land for her **wrestling!** Any man who wanted to marry her had to wrestle with her and win, or pay a forfeit of 100 horses. At thirty, she was still a spinster, but she did own 10,000 horses...

One of the largest and most complicated crosswords ever published took 7½ years to complete, has over 6,000 clues and has never been completely solved by anyone.

It would seem that even ghosts don't go on forever, the average 'life-span' is 400 years. However, there is an exception to this, in the form of a Roman centurion, who is reputed to have been haunting Strood, in Essex for the past fifteen and a half centuries.

The Japanese aren't just famous for their cars, but for their railways too. In fact, their trains are the busiest in the world. So many people use them, especially at rush hour times that professional **pushers** are employed to squash the passengers into the carriages, clear of the doors, before they are closed.

When Dauphin Louis Antoine became King Louis XIX, it was to become the shortest reign on record. He abdicated in favour of Henri V after just fifteen minutes!

AN INTRODUCTION TO THE KRANKIES

THE KRANKIES—husband and wife comedy team Ian and Janette Krankie, with a little help from their 'offspring' wee Jimmy Krankie—are now readily acknowledged as a show-stopping act in clubs and theatres. And, in the last couple of years they have made a huge impact on television.

Their latest and most important success has come with the BBC TV 'Crackerjack' series, in which wee Jimmy Krankie, as portrayed by 4 ft 5 ins tall Janette, has become the undisputed 'champion' of children throughout the country.

Their TV breakthrough on 'Crackerjack' is just reward for Ian and Janette, who have built-up their TV popularity since they shot to national prominence following a show-stopping debut in The Royal Variety Show. Now they are very much TV properties—thanks to a blend of humour, singing and pure entertainment that is unique to them. And of course they have an hilarious ally in wee Jimmy!

The twosome (or threesome) have been together for several years now, and despite their current success rate, there is no way in which The Krankies can be described as 'overnight stars.'

They have been star names for over a decade as live entertainers, and are readily acknowledged as one of the biggest club and theatre attractions in the country. The success they have achieved on stage is now paying dividends on television, and 'Crackerjack' is the breakthrough for which they have long been striving.

Prior to 'Crackerjack' they achieved national prominence when they became undisputed hits of the Royal Variety Show. Overnight, the two Scottish performers, with a little help from 'wee Jimmy' became national favourites.

Now they have consolidated their success as TV entertainers and continue to be huge attractions in clubs and the theatre.

Ian and Janette have been together for over a decade. They first met during a pantomime season at the Pavilion Theatre, Glasgow. Janette was then making her debut as a dancer, while Ian was employed as the theatre electrician.

"We were both making our start in life," says Janette. "I had given up my job as a shorthand typist for a chance of a showbiz career, and Ian was only working as an electrician because he hoped he could persuade someone to give him a chance on stage.

"So we had something in common, and our initial friendship blossomed into romance. It also led to us forming an impromptu singing and dancing act, and by the time the season ended we also found that by messing around, we could make people laugh."

And so, as The Krankies, they began their push for stardom as local club entertainers. It was a slow process, and after marrying two years after their initial meeting, they moved to the North-East. It was there that they had their grounding in club entertainment.

"We were working practically every day of the week," says Ian, "but we still found time to work on the act. Eventually comedy became the mainstay—as it is today—but we have always retained the singing and dancing so that our audiences can have a complete show."

With this policy The Krankies rapidly built-up a reputation and soon they were travelling all over the country. It meant another move to a central base, so they settled in Coventry—where they still live.

The Royal Variety Show changed their lives completely, and it came immediately after they had won the award for being clubland's Top Comedy Act.

Today, their career has been enhanced still further by the 'Crackerjack' series and The Krankies are stars in the truest sense of the word.

Ian and Janette have proven conclusively that there is no substitute for talent. And their well deserved success—aided of course by 'wee Jimmy'—couldn't have happened to two nicer people.

PANTOMIME

INTRODUCTION

The play at the end of every Crackerjack programme is always very popular and very funny to watch—but have you ever thought of getting together with a few friends and putting on a play of your own?

It can be great fun, practising the lines, rehearsing together, collecting the props (those are the bits and pieces you'll need on stage) and the costumes, of course. You can make it as simple or as complicated as you like, but you'll be surprised at what you can accomplish, once you get started.

Pantomime is a smashing thing for beginners. They are supposed to be funny and if something goes wrong and your audience laughs, so much the better—you might even decide to leave that bit in at the next performance!

Just to get you started on some ideas of your own, here's a script for a Cinderella pantomime, you might want to alter it to suit yourselves or follow it word for word, it depends on your circumstances. If you have a very small cast, you could cut out a couple of parts, say those of the Prince's manservant, the stepmother, or Buttons. On the other hand, if you've got people clamouring for parts in your panto, introduce a few more parts. They could be non-speaking ones, like having a few dancers at the ball.

Cinderella has been chosen specially as a starting off point, simply because it is a story that almost everybody knows. But there may be some of your audience who don't know the story, especially the younger ones and from this point of view it is a good idea to have a story-teller, or narrator. This is also a good ploy to use, if you want someone to keep the audience's attention whilst you're changing the scenery, or if you feel there are some parts of the panto which you feel are too difficult to attempt with your limited resources.

Anyway, give it a try, you never know how easy it could be, until you do...

CINDERELLA

CAST

In order of appearance

NARRATOR	the story teller
CINDERELLA	a young girl, dressed in rags
STEPMOTHER	Cinderella's stepmother
BUTTONS	a faithful servant and Cinderella's friend
TAPIOCA GORGONZOLA	the ugly Sisters
FAIRY GODMOTHER	Cinderella's fairy godmother
PRINCE	Who invites everyone to a Ball at the Palace
MANWELLI	The Prince's incompetent manservant

SETS

1. The kitchen at Cinderella's home
2. A corner of the Great Hall at the Prince's palace

SCENE 1 CINDERELLA'S KITCHEN EARLY IN THE MORNING

The kitchen is a dark and gloomy place. Cinderella is just putting the finishing touches to the fire in the hearth. Then she begins to lay the table for breakfast. She is dressed in very old and tattered clothes. The narrator stands to one side of the stage…

NARRATOR: Let me introduce you to our heroine, Cinderella. This is how her morning begins. Up at five every morning, clean out the grate, get the breakfast…Work, work, work from dawn to dusk. I really am going to get that girl to join a union. At least then she'll get teabreaks. But look out! Here comes the dragon—her stepmother, that is, now you'll see what we all have to put up with…

STEPMOTHER: Is that table not set yet! The birds have been singing for hours, keeping me from my beauty sleep and not so much as a bowl of Snap Crackle and Pop on the table…

CINDERELLA: Oh, but…

STEPMOTHER: Don't give me any excuses, you're a lazy good-for-nothing, just like your father. I don't know why I ever married him, other than the fact that my two beautiful darlings needed a daddy to call their own.

NARRATOR: Own! Their own *daddy* joined the Foreign Legion, just to get away from them!

STEPMOTHER: Still, that's enough of that. Get that table finished and I'll go and call my darlings….(exits, calling) TAPIOCA! GORGONZOLA!

NARRATOR: Voice like the Whitstable foghorn that woman, I don't know how Cinderella puts up with it. But shh! She's coming back.

STEPMOTHER: (PUSHING HER TWO DAUGHTERS ALONG IN FRONT OF HER). Come along you two, come along! You're not going to find husbands lying in bed all day and anyway you both need a good breakfast. Tapioca, (TALKING TO HER FAT DAUGHTER) You're looking quite peaky, dear, I think you'd better have two bowls of porridge, this morning!

TAPIOCA: (SULKING) But I don't like porridge, it's all lumpy.

GORGONZOLA: Just the thing for you sister dear, it matches your figure!

TAPIOCA: Huh! You're only jealous, tin ribs! If it wasn't for your big head, you'd slip through the cracks in the floorboards…

STEPMOTHER: Girls! Girls! Sit down to breakfast this minute. (THEY ALL BEGIN TO EAT VERY NOISILY)

NARRATOR: I reckon if they had a 'Hog of the Year Show', they'd have difficulty choosing between these two. But hang on, who's coming. Oh, it's only Cinderella's friend, Buttons…

BUTTONS: Excuse me, Madam. A messenger from the palace has just called with this. (BUTTONS PROFFERS A LARGE MESSAGE, ROLLED UP AND TIED WITH RIBBON).

STEPMOTHER: (SNATCHING THE MESSAGE FROM BUTTONS) Well, don't just stand there! Let me see it, let me see it!

TAPIOCA: It's probably just a message to say that he's noticed my great beauty and he would like to marry me.

GORGONZOLA: It's probably a message to say that he's noticed your great weight and he'd like you to visit his vineyards to tread his grapes.

STEPMOTHER: Girls! Girls! Do stop squabbling and listen. It's an invitation to everyone in the house to attend a Grand Ball. The Prince has decided to marry and he is hoping to meet his future bride there.

GORGONZOLA: Oh, how exciting, how spiffing, how, how…positively splendidiferous…

TAPIOCA: Oh, do stop spitting and spluttering! Come on, we'll have to start our preparations now, if we're going to look our best!

BUTTONS: (MUTTERING) Polyfilla and plastic masks couldn't make **them** look any better! (LOUDER) You said **everyone,** Madam. Does that mean that Cinderella and I can go to the Ball, too?

STEPMOTHER: You! Go to the Ball! I can't believe you're serious. I'm sure the Prince has quite enough servants of his own! There will be lots of work for you two to do here. You'll be far to busy to go to the Ball! (SHE SWEEPS OUT).

CINDERELLA: Never mind, Buttons. you tried. And anyway I'm sure we wouldn't really enjoy that silly ball. (SHE LOOKS DISAPPOINTED) And what would I wear? I haven't had a new dress since my silly father married that woman!

BUTTONS: Oh, I don't mind for myself, Cinderella, only for you. I'm sure that the Prince would fall in love with you the moment he saw you…

END OF ACT ONE

SCENE 2
CINDERELLA'S KITCHEN A FEW DAYS LATER

NARRATOR: You've no idea what it's been like this last few days! World War 3 would be like a Sunday School outing after this. Bring me! Fetch me! Carry me! And the arguing! Well, I've just had to cover my ears once or twice. How poor Cinderella has put up with them all, I just don't know. Oh no! Here they come again…

TAPIOCA: But you promised! You said that if I was wearing the purple, you'd wear the orange or the green. If you wear that pink, we'll look like a bunch of grapes, seasick ones!

GORGONZOLA: You only want me to wear the green because you know it doesn't suit my colouring…

TAPIOCA: Colouring! Colouring! I've seen more colouring on a zebra crossing! You're just jealous of my beauty. Anyway, where's that wretched Cinderella, I've got a hundred things for her to do, I'm never going to be ready in time. CINDERELLA! CINDERELLA!
ENTER CINDERELLA. LOOKING HARASSED AND OVERWORKED.

GORGONZOLA: Have you filled the bath with goats milk, as I instructed you?

CINDERELLA: Yes, Gorgonzola.

TAPIOCA: Don't bother taking the goats out. She'll never notice the difference the way she smells. And if you think I'm going in that dress you chose, you can think again. It makes me look like a pair of curtains…

GORGONZOLA: Well, pull yourself together then!

THE UGLY SISTERS EXIT, STILL ARGUING. BUTTONS ENTERS TO FIND CINDERELLA CRYING.

BUTTONS: Oh, don't cry, Cinders. I'm sure it will be a rotten old Ball anyway. Especially with those two and that old bat their mother, there.

CINDERELLA: Oh, it's not really that, Buttons. It's just that I wish they could be a little bit kind to me sometimes. My father's so busy working to pay for their new hats and gowns, he doesn't have time to notice how horrid they are.

BUTTONS: I know. It used to be so nice before they came to live here. I can't think what your father was thinking about when he married her, his mind must have been wandering.

CINDERELLA: Yes, and I sometimes think that it has got lost altogether. (THEY BOTH LAUGH).

BUTTONS: Hush! I think I can hear them leaving at last…

TAPIOCA: (FROM OFFSTAGE) We must fly, we're going to be late!

BUTTONS: (PRETENDING TO SHOUT) Don't forget your broomsticks!

CINDERELLA: (LAUGHS).

BUTTONS: That's better! You look much nicer when you laugh. In fact, you look happier altogether…

FAIRY GODMOTHER: (WHO HAS ENTERED QUIETLY, WHILST THEY WERE TALKING). I can make you happier still, Cinderella, if you will let me…

CINDERELLA: Who are you? How long have you been there?

FAIRY GODMOTHER: All your life my dear, although you've never seen me before. But enough of that, do you want to go to this Ball or not.

CINDERELLA: (WISTFULLY) Yes, yes I would, but how? I've nothing to wear and I can't possibly get to the Palace now…

FAIRY GODMOTHER: Just leave all of that up to me. Buttons, I'll need your help. Go out into the garden and pick the largest pumpkin that you can find. Beside it put six white mice.

BUTTONS: (OFFSTAGE, PAUSES SLIGHTLY THEN CALLS). Yes, I've done everything. Oh! Oh! I don't believe it!

FAIRY GODMOTHER: Now find me three black rats…(SHE LOOKS OFFSTAGE) Yes, those will do nicely. (SHE WAVES HER ARMS, AS IF TO CAST A MAGIC SPELL). Perfect! You can look now, Cinderella.

CINDERELLA: (CINDERELLA LOOKS OFFSTAGE AND GASPS IN AMAZEMENT) A gold coach drawn by six white horses! For me?

BUTTONS: (RUSHING IN) And a coachman in black livery, with two footmen at the back.

FAIRY GODMOTHER: And now for you, my dear. It is time for your transformation. Come with me. (EXIT OFFSTAGE, CINDERELLA MEEKLY FOLLOWING HER GODMOTHER).

BUTTONS: I'ts just like a dream, I can't believe it's happening. But I wonder where they've got to?

(BUTTONS BEGINS TO PACE THE FLOOR, PAUSING TO PEEP OFFSTAGE ONCE OR TWICE UNTIL CINDERELLA REAPPEARS).

BUTTONS: Oh, Cinderella, you look beautiful!

FAIRY GODMOTHER: Hurry along now Cinderella, you're going to be very late. (CINDERELLA RUSHES OFFSTAGE).

CINDERELLA: Goodbye, goodbye.

FAIRY GODMOTHER: Don't forget Cinderella, you must be back by midnight. For as the clock chimes twelve my spell will end.

END OF SCENE TWO

SCENE 3
THE PALACE GRAND HALL
LATER THAT EVENING

NARRATOR: Cinderella could hardly believe her good fortune. The Prince danced with her the whole evening. Tapioca and Gorgonzola were green with envy. In that green dress, Gorgonzola looked like the Jolly Green Giant!

CINDERELLA: I...I really must be going soon. I haven't to be late home.

PRINCE: Can't you stay a little longer? Just one more dance.

CINDERELLA: (THE CLOCK BEGINS TO CHIME, CINDERELLA LOOKS HORRIFIED. SHE RUSHES OFFSTAGE, DISAPPEARING AS THE CLOCK CHIMES TWELVE).

PRINCE: NO! NO! Stop! Bring her back someone. (THE PRINCE'S MANSERVANT RUSHES AFTER HER, RETURNING A MOMENT LATER CARRYING A LARGE BLACK WELLINGTON).

PRINCE: Manwelli, What is this?

MANWELLI: A Wellie, your lordship sir. (MANWELLI SPEAKS WITH A FOREIGN ACCENT). I found it on the steps, the young lady must have dropped it!

NARRATOR: It's all to do with inflation, you know. Who can afford glass slippers, these days?

PRINCE: Tomorrow I will take this slipper...er, I mean wellie to every house in the kingdom and whichever lady it fits, I will marry.

END OF SCENE THREE

SCENE 4
BACK IN CINDERELLA'S KITCHEN
THE NEXT DAY

TAPIOCA: (TAPPING HER FOOT IMPATIENTLY) You'd think the Prince would be here by now, wouldn't you Mummy?

STEPMOTHER: Patience my dear, patience.

GORGONZOLA: I don't know what you're worrying about. Your shoes are like coal barges. Put wheels on them and you could do tours around the Widdecombe Rubbish Tips…

TAPIOCA: That does it! (SHE AND GORGONZOLA BEGIN TO FIGHT. THEN THERE IS A LOUD KNOCK AT THE DOOR).

STEPMOTHER: Stop it! Stop it at once. There's someone here. Tapioca! Pull in your stomach and try to look presentable. Gorgonzola, curl up your toes, that way you might just get on that boot!

BUTTONS: (ENTERS WITH THE PRINCE AND MANWELLI. MANWELLI HAS THE BOOT ON A CUSHION) His Royal Highness.
(EVERYONE BOWS TO THE PRINCE).

PRINCE: (LOOKING DOUBTFULLY AT THE UGLY SISTERS. Erm, (COUGHS LOUDLY) Yours is the last house in the kingdom and I haven't found anyone who the boot fits.

TAPIOCA: Let me try it, Your Highness. I'm sure I won't disappoint you. (THE PRINCE PULLS A FACE AND THEN LOOKS RELIEVED AS TAPIOCA GIVES UP STRUGGLING TO GET THE BOOT ON.

GORGONZOLA: Perhaps if you tried the G fitting, my dear, (SHE GLANCES IN A SUPERIOR WAY AT HER SISTER). Let me try it on, my feet have always been much daintier than yours. (SHE REMOVES HER SHOE WITH A FLOURISH).

TAPIOCA: Now you know why they call her *Gorgonzola!*
(SHE STRUGGLES HARD, BUT SHE CANNOT MAKE THE BOOT FIT).

PRINCE: What are we to do Manwelli, will I never have a matching set?

BUTTONS: Do not despair, your majesty. There is still one person who has not tried on the boot. (BUTTONS GOES OFFSTAGE AND RETURNS WITH CINDERELLA).

PRINCE: (THE PRINCE LOOKS AT CINDERELLA CLOSELY). Will you try on the boot?

CINDERELLA: (NODDING MEEKLY) Yes, your Royal Highness. (THE BOOT SLIPS ON EASILY).

PRINCE: My love!

CINDERELLA: My Prince! (THEY EMBRACE).

THE UGLY SISTERS: UGH! My Heart! (THE UGLY SISTERS FALL IN A HEAP, CLUTCHING THEIR HEARTS).

NARRATOR: And they all lived happily ever after. Well nearly all of them…and at least for part of the time…

THE END.

FROM STUDIO TO SCREEN

Have you ever wondered how that picture and the sounds actually get on to your television set, for a programme like **Crackerjack** for example? Well, there's certainly a good deal more to it than the actual pictures and sounds that find their way into your home.

The studios themselves are huge, about the size of an aeroplane hangar, not very exotic or exciting as they are, but they can become almost anything that the set designer would like them to become. For a programme like **Crackerjack,** however, which relies on a live audience for its 'atmosphere', the studio is slightly different. It is the BBC TV Theatre at Shepherd's Bush, where the audience can be a part of the show, as well as the entertainers.

Once the shows have been planned and the scripts written, the stage designer can move in. He plans the scenery and how the show will look. Then the carpentry department and the painters go to work, building and painting all the things that you will see on the show. Pale colours are used, because colour cameras make things look much brighter than they really are.

Meanwhile, in the Wardrobe department, the Wardrobe mistress and her staff are making sure that all the clothes that will be needed for the programme will be ready on time—and that includes making sure that they are cleaned and pressed. Special costumes are often hired, if they are only to be used once, although the BBC have vast wardrobe stocks of their own.

Rehearsals have to take place, too. Where the programme's actors or presenters run through the show and it may take several practices before it is good enough for an audience to see.

The lighting is a crucial part of presenting a television programme. The powerful lights have to be carefully checked before the programme is recorded, the lighting engineers don't want anything to go wrong with them once the cameras are rolling.

Television cameras are fixed on to a 'dolly', which is a kind of trolley, on which they can move along very quietly. Some dollys have seats on them too, which can elevate the camera man up above the action so that he can get overhead shots as well.

But it's not just the pictures which are important to television, there is the sound to consider as well. There are all different kinds of microphones which can be used, depending on the kind of production.

There are the simple ones which just hang from the ceiling or are on a stand and there are some which hang from extending arms which in turn are attached to trolleys, in much the same way as some cameras are. These are called *booms*. But for productions where the presenters or the actors have to move about a lot, there are tiny microphones which are equipped with tiny radio transmitters, which can be clipped to a person's clothing. These also have their own power pack, which is usually hidden in a back pocket.

All the equipment in the studio is connected to a sound-proofed room nearby, where there are a number of monitors, speakers and numerous switches and buttons and a variety of people to operate them. This is where you would usually find the Director, the Editor and various engineers. Each camera is linked to a monitor screen, and it is in this room that it is decided which 'shots' and 'angles' you will see at home. Nowadays, it is possible, through electronic wizardry, to show you things on your screen that weren't really there at all.

If a programme is to be recorded and shown on television at a later date, all the pictures and sound are recorded on tape. If, however, it is a live programme, the sounds and pictures are sent direct from the studio through the cables to various transmitters masts throughout the country. From the transmitter masts they travel on radio waves to be picked up by your television aerial, to pass along the cable and into your television set.

So that you can sit in the comfort of your sitting room to watch something which may be happening hundreds of miles away.

TAKE A LETTER

See if you can answer each of these questions. There's one for each letter of the alphabet.

A. ABRACADABRA is a magic word used by magicians, but what did it start out life as?

B. BANANA trees aren't really trees at all. What are they?

C. CRABS. Which are the smallest species in the world?

D. DOGS. Which breed of dogs were named after a famous King? *King Charles*

E. ELEPHANT. Which elephants have the largest ears, Indian ones or African ones? *African.*

F. FLAGS. Which country was the first to introduce a national flag and when?

G. GOLD. Where does most of the world's gold come from?

H. HOVERCRAFT. Who invented it?

I. INSECTS. How many species are there in Great Britain?
(a) over 10,000
(b) over 20,000
(c) over 30,000

J. JELLYFISH. Which is the most poisonous?

K. KANGAROO is an aborigine word, what does it mean?

L. LEPIDOPTERA. Which animals belong to this group?

M. MILE. Where did the word mile originate?

N. NUGGET. What is one?

O. OCTOPUS. What is the largest one in the world?

P. PANCAKES. One particular day is especially thought of in connection with pancakes, what is its correct title?

Q. QUEEN. Which English queen has had the shortest reign in history?

R. RICKSHAW. What is a rickshaw and where would you be most likely to find one?

S. SKELETON. How many bones are there in an adult, human skeleton?

T. TEDDY BEARS. Who were they named after?

U. USSR. By what name is this country more commonly known?

V. VOLCANO. Where is the world's highest, active volcano?

W. WATCH. When, and by whom, was the first pocket watch invented.

X. XENOPHOBIA. What is this a fear of?

Y. YO-YO. Where did the yo-yo originate?

Z. ZIGGURAT. What is a ziggurat?

Answers on page 77

ROLLER COASTER

Join in all the thrills and spills of the fair. Loop the loop and beat all your friends to the Finish.

This is a game for up to six players. You will need a dice and a different coloured counter or button for each person playing.

START

1
2
CANDY FLOSS IN EYE. GO BACK 2 SQUARES
4
5
6
7 GO ON THREE SQUARES
9
10
11 THROW AGAIN!
13
14 HATS BLOW OFF BACK TO 9
16
17

PLACES NEAR AND FAR

Here's a chance to test your geography. Groan, Groan. Well, not so much a test, more of a quick imaginary trip to places near and far. Try it and see…

1. Balmoral, what is it and where is it.

2. It used to be called Miklagard, what is it called now?

3. What are Liverpudlians, Mancunians and Glaswegians?

4. These are all capital cities, of where?
a New York b Wellington c Ottawa
d Canberra

5. In which sea would you find it impossible to sink and why?

6. Where would you find the pyramids?

7. Where would you find Canarvon and where would you find Caernarvon?

8. A volcanic island appeared off the coast of Iceland in 1963, what is it called?

9. Which is the largest country in the world?

10. Where would you find the following towns and cities?
a Calais b San Sebastian c Exeter
d Munich

Answers on page 77

NOT QUITE RIGHT!

How observant are you? Each of the items on this page has something missing or something wrong with it. Can you spot the deliberate mistakes?

SHAPE UP

1. Five of these six shapes will fit together to form a circle, the other is spare. Which one is it?
2. How many sides have each of the following shapes:
   (a) rectangle
   (b) octagon
   (c) trilateral
3. Which countries do these outline maps show?

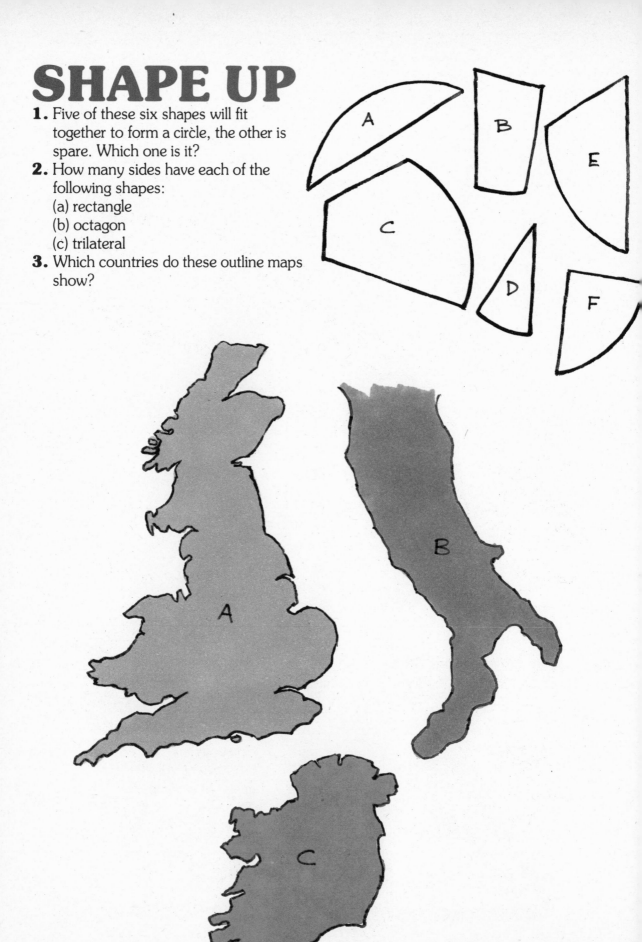

4. From which trees do each of these leaves come?

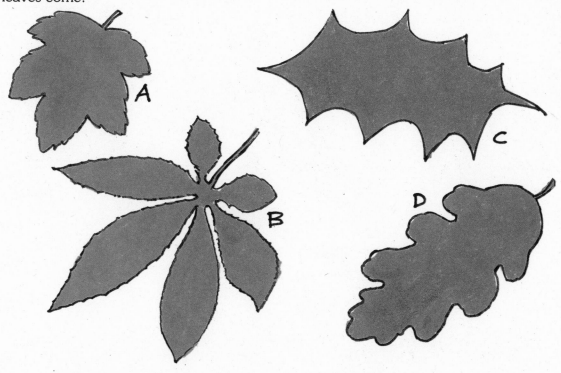

5. These are common traffic signs. What do they mean?

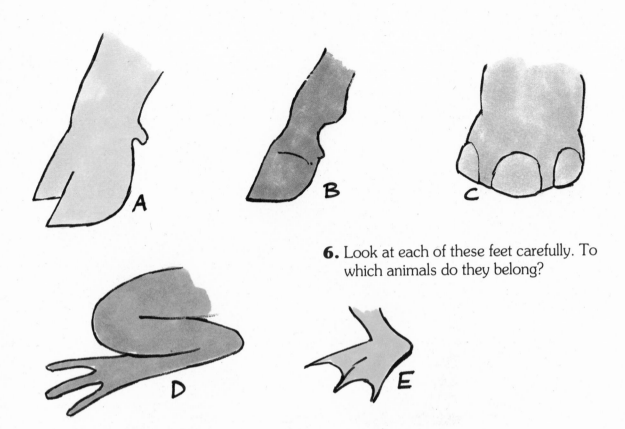

6. Look at each of these feet carefully. To which animals do they belong?

7. These are all outlines of well-known nursery rhyme figures. Do you know who they are?

WHICH IS WHICH

How much do you know about dinosaurs? Can you match up the correct names from the list with the correct animal?

1. STEGOSAURUS.

2. DIMETRODON

3. DIPLODOCUS

4. PTERANODON

5. TYRANNOSAURUS

Answers on page 77

All Tied Up

When Stu and the Krankies tried out this Houdini act, they hadn't reckoned on getting in such a tangle. Can you sort out who has the padlock and get them out of this mess?

DO YOU KNOW?

1. What is the **Amanita phalloides?** To give you a clue; it's very, very poisonous!
2. What were the **Hindenberg** and the **Zeppelin?**
3. **The New York Times** is the thickest one in the world. What is it?
4. **Saluki, Lowchen** and **Chihuahua** are all types of what?
5. The first person that God created, according to the bible.
6. John Lennon was a member of this famous group, what was it called?
7. They form the largest animal group on earth, what are they?
8. The winner of the men's Decathlon in the 1980 Olympic Games in Russia?
9. **Atlantic, Pacific** and **Indian** are all names of what?
10. This word is used in relation to the sun and its power, what is it?
11. **Lloyds** of London are famous for what?
12. The first letter of each of the answers to the questions on this page spell out a favourite **Crackerjack** word, what is it?

Answers on page 77

BUILD YOUR OWN CONCORDE

A flight on Concorde is way beyond the means of most of us, but as a slight consolation prize, you might like to have a go at making your own paper version. Here's the basic model, but there's nothing to stop you adding a few modifications of your own…

You will need:
a sheet of paper 28 cm by 22 cm.
1 paper clip.
1 staple (optional).

Instructions

1. Fold the sheet of paper in half widthways, then lay it down flat, with the crease facing up to you.

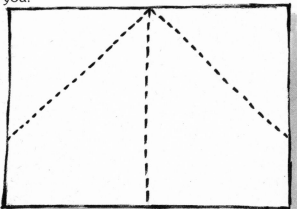

2. Fold over the corners, so that they lap over at the centre fold.

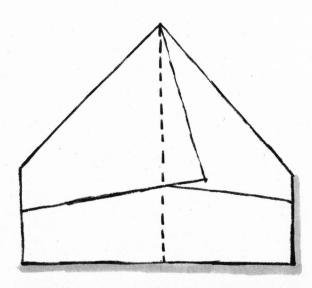

3. Re-fold the sheet along the centre line and fold the sides back, making these folds about 2½ cm from the centre fold on either side. Staple (if you have one) as in the diagram.

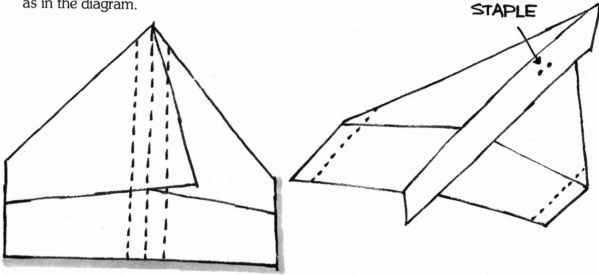

STAPLE

4. Cut off a small portion of the point and bend the edges of the wings as shown. Secure the paper clip to the nose.

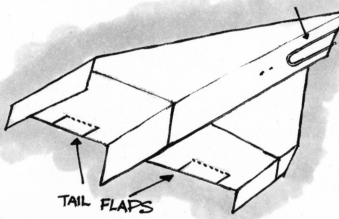

PAPER CLIP

TAIL FLAPS

5. Make four small snips in the tail section of the plane and then turn the right way up. Bend up the tail flaps as shown in the diagram. These will control the upward flight of the plane and its rolling action, so experiment with them for the best effect.
HAPPY FLYING!

MYSTERIOUS MAGIC

How would you like to astound your friends with your magical powers? Well, with a little practise and a little behind-the-scenes preparation, you can, and it won't be too hard...

Quick Change

No self-respecting magician would be without a handkerchief that changes colour and I'm sure that you won't want to be either! You'll need two squares of silk of different colours (red and blue, green and yellow, or patterned and plain) and a needle and thread...and someone who's good at sewing, if you're not! You will also need a small metal curtain ring, which should be just big enough to pull the double thickness of the material through.

Now, lay one square of silk directly on top of the other square and secure with a couple of stitches right in the centre. Then fold the squares diagonally across as shown, stitching along the right-hand side, leaving one inch at the top unstitched. Cut off this corner and fold the edges down, sewing the curtain ring between them. This must be done very neatly, so that it will not be noticed.

To prepare the handkerchief for a public appearance, take corner B of the inner square and pull it up on the inside, so that you can just see, and hold the corner, through the curtain ring. You can hold the handkerchief up by this corner and it will look quite normal and a quick tug on the hidden corner, will turn the whole thing inside out, thereby **changing** the colour.

The secret of this trick is to do the whole thing very quickly. Pull the handkerchief out of your pocket, change the colour and put it straight back into your pocket. Your audience won't be able to believe their eyes...

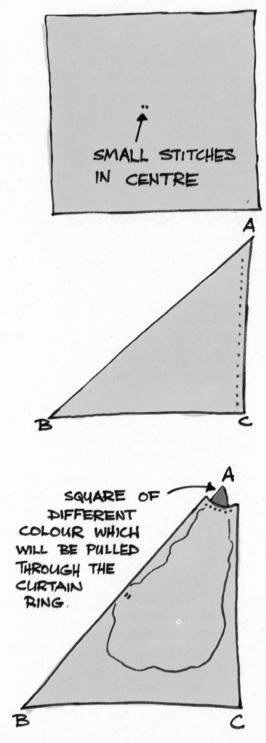

SMALL STITCHES IN CENTRE

SQUARE OF DIFFERENT COLOUR WHICH WILL BE PULLED THROUGH THE CURTAIN RING.

The Vanishing Hankie

You might need a bit of help with the props for this trick. You'll need a small square of silk (about the size of a handkerchief), a clear plastic tumbler with a small hole drilled in the side, a square of cloth to cover the tumbler completely and a jug of water. The hole in the tumbler should be large enough to pull the 'handkerchief' through, but small enough to cover with your thumb, so that the water does not leak out when it is filled.

The first stage of the trick is to fill the tumbler full of water, making sure that your thumb is firmly over the hole. This proves that it is a perfectly **ordinary** tumbler, of course. Then pour the water back into the jug, or drink it if you're thirsty, and dry the tumbler. Now arrange the silk square in the tumbler, allowing one of its corners to poke through the hole and grip this with your thumb, but don't let anyone see you! Secure another square of cloth over the top of the tumbler with an elastic band and then hold your hands up so that everyone can see that they're quite empty.

Now comes the tricky part, which you'll have to practise a bit. Reach under the cloth and pull out the silk square very quickly, holding it up for everyone to see. Then, remove the elastic band and cover from the tumbler, so that everyone can see that it has really escaped from the tumbler.

If you want to be really flashy, you can then refill the tumbler with water again and, just to prove what an **ordinary** one it is! But don't forget to empty it again immediately—a leaking glass could give the whole game away…

The Disappearing Penny

This is a fairly easy trick to perform. You're going to make a penny disappear from your hand—a penny that wasn't really there in the first place! You'll need several coins in your pocket and make sure that you know exactly what you're going to say. Something like: "To perform this trick I need a penny, I think I have one in here somewhere." Then take out all the coins, selecting a penny and holding it up for your audience to see. you then say: "I'll just put the rest back." You do this and you also slip the penny back in amongst the other coins without anyone else noticing. Put your finger and thumb (as though you were still holding the coin) into your other hand, as if to leave the penny there.

Now here's the really convincing part. Get somebody to hold your wrist firmly, to prevent the **penny** from slipping up your sleeve or anywhere else. Then mutter the magic works (abracadabra, will always do if you can't think of anything else) and then open your hand and of course, there isn't anything there. If you practise this a few times in private first, you should be able to amaze your audience quite easily.

GIVE US A CLUE

This is not just a test of your knowledge, it's a test of your maths, too!

Each question is followed by two clues. If you can answer the question, without using either of the clues and you get the answer right, you score the maximum—10. If, however, you use one clue, you only score 6 out of 10 and if you have to use both of the clues, you only score 4 out of 10. You don't score anything for wrong answers, of course, no matter how hard you tried!

See how many you can can score out of a possible 100.

1. Though he looks like a bear, he is actually a member of the raccoon family.
   (a) His windpipe is covered with a special horny layer, as a protection against the bamboo canes which he likes to eat.
   (b) He is a favourite with the Chinese.

2 He was born in Tennessee, became a hero of the Wild West and an American Congressman.
   (a) When confronted by both a grizzly bear and a panther at the same time, he is reputed to have split a rock into two pieces with one rifle shot, killing both animals with the flying splinters.
   (b) His unusual hat made him easily recognizable.

3. You would be most unlikely to see this in the sky at mid-day or midnight?
   (a) It is caused by the sunlight shining through drops of rain.
   (b) It is said that there is a pot of gold at the end of it.

4. He's a pantomime character, who is always to be found in the east?
   (a) His worst enemy is his uncle.
   (b) He was saved by a lamp.

5. He lives in Australia and likes to sleep all day?
   (a) His relatives are sometimes called Boomers and Blue Flyers.
   (b) He lives in the trees, but his larger relatives prefer the wide open spaces.

6. Invented by Thomas Edison when he was experimenting with sound?
  (a) Pop music could never have become as popular without their invention.
  (b) The name has changed, but the purpose remains the same.

7. This animal isn't a horse, but it is ridden in races.
  (a) One of its eggs is large enough to make an omelette for twelve men.
  (b) It is the largest one of its kind in the world.

8. During hot weather these animals sweat through their paws.
  (a) They also have fleshy 'gums' which act as toothbrushes, cleaning the animal's teeth whenever he opens or closes his mouth.
  (b) They are very common pets.

9. There are over 2,000 species of this plant which is said to have many special properties including:
  (a) In the seventeenth century in England, it was put in fishponds, to cure sick fish.
  (b) If eaten after garlic, it will take the smell away.

10. Where would you find enough fat to make seven bars of soap?
  (a) In the same place, you would find 350 bones in a very young sample, and 206 bones in an older one.
  (b) Here also, you would find enough carbon to make the lead for 9,000 pencils.

Answers on page 77

ON THE RIGHT TRACK

See if you're on the right track with this quiz. Ten points for each correct answer.

1. How did nylon get its name?

2. Which is the highest mountain in the United Kingdom?

3. What is a quadruped?

4. Where does the sea-horse keep its young?

5. Which of these answers is true? An eclipse is caused by;

a The moon being between the sun and the earth.

b The sun being between the earth and the moon.

c The earth being between the sun and the moon.

6. Which King was known as the 'Merry Monarch'?

7. Which comes first, the thunder or the lightning?

8. Finish this famous proverb 'Honesty…'

9. Who was the Greek who was reputed to have shouted 'Eureka' on discovering the principle of specific gravity whilst in his bath?

10. Little John fought with him and then became his friend. Who was he?

ANSWERS:

1. It was discovered in **NEW YORK** and **LONDON** at about the same time.

2. Ben Nevis.

3. A four-footed animal.

4. In a pouch.

5. (a) this causes an eclipse of the sun. (b) this could not cause an eclipse, because the sun is too far away from the moon to come between it and the earth. (c) this causes an eclipse of the moon.

6. Charles II.

7. Lightning.

8. …is the best policy.

9. Archimedes.

10. Robin Hood.

MATCHING PAIRS

Look carefully at the twelve pictures here and then see if you can match them up into six pairs.

STU AT THE ZOO

Here are a few rib-tickling jokes to try out on your friends…

What's black and white, black and white, black and white, black and white, black and white…
A penguin rolling down a hill.

Why did they cross a pigeon with a woodpecker?
So that he could knock on the door when he delivered the messages.

Why wouldn't they let the butterfly into the dance?
Because it was a moth ball.

Which bird can lift the heaviest weights?
A crane, of course.

Which game do crocodiles like to play best of all?
Snap!

Why do leopards never escape from the zoo?
Because they're always spotted.

What did the mother glow-worm say to the father glow-worm?
I think our boy's very bright for his age.

AMAZED

Stu Francis has managed to get lost in the maze of corridors in the B.B.C. Can you help him find his way to the Crackerjack studios?

WOULD IT WORK?

Brains scrubbed and at the ready! Here are some ticklish problems to solve, or you might just like to make a guess at the answers…

1. During a holiday afloat, The Krankies, Stu and some friends came to a sudden halt when the wind fell out of their sails. They were just reaching for the oars when Stu came up with a brilliant idea, or so he thought. "If we all blow at once, I'm sure we've got enough puff to get this thing movin' again."
WAS HE RIGHT, OR DID THEY ALL GET VERY TIRED ARMS ROWING HOME?

2. The one thing that Stu dreaded was having to swim home. "I'll sink like a stone!" he wailed. "Never mind," comforted Jimmy, "the water's very cold, you'll sink more slowly, at least!"
WAS SHE RIGHT? DO THINGS SINK MORE SLOWLY IN COLD WATER THAN THEY DO IN WARM WATER?

3. Stu stared dolefully at a small piece of wood floating by the boat. "We'll just get washed in to the shore," he said hopefully. "Not a chance," replied one of the Krankies, 'we're too far from land for that, without anything to push us forward, we'll stay here for days, forever come to that…"
WHO WAS RIGHT?

Answers on page 77

SIX OF THE BEST!

Funnies to make the day pass more quickly, or to take the pain away when you wish you hadn't got out of bed at all…

Biology teacher: We've learned that we breathe in oxygen in the daytime, who can tell me what we breathe at night?

Jimmy: Nitrogen, Miss?

Teacher: Name four members of the dog family for me.

Girl: Mother dog, Father dog, Brother dog and Sister dog.

Teacher: I wish you'd pay a little attention, you might learn something.

Johnny: I'm paying as little as I can.

Mum: Well Jane, what does the teacher think of your schoolwork?

Jane: I think she likes it, she always puts a little kiss at the bottom of the page.

Maths teacher: Will somebody in the class give me a sentence with the word 'centimetre' in it?

Danny: I will, Miss. Erm…My little sister was late coming home from school and I was centimetre.

Teacher: This will not do, Charlie! You must learn to give and take.

Charlie: I have learn't, sir. I gave him a kick on the ankle and then I took his crisps.

THE KRANKIES GUIDE TO KNOCK-KNOCK KNOCKING

Knock, Knock.
Who's there?
Ivor.
Ivor Who?
Ivor you let me in the door, or I'll climb in through the window.

Knock, Knock.
Who's there?
Lettuce.
Lettuce who?
Lettuce in and you'll soon find out.

Knock, Knock.
Who's there?
Doctor.
Doctor who?
That's right.

Knock, Knock.
Who's there?
Cook.
Cook who?
That's the first one I've heard this year.

Knock, Knock.
Who's there?
Scot.
Scot who?
Scot nothing to do with you.

Knock, Knock.
Who's there?
Alison.
Alison who?
Alison to my radio all the time.

Knock, Knock.
Who's there?
Martini.
Martini who?
Martini hands are frozen.

Knock, Knock.
Who's there?
Somebody who can't reach your blinkin' doorbell.

Knock, Knock.
Who's there?
Watson.
Watson who?
Watson the televisión after Crackerjack's finished?

Knock, Knock.
Who's there?
Dismay.
Dismay who?
Dismay be a joke to you, but it doesn't make me laugh.

REMEMBER, REMEMBER...

So, you think your memory is pretty good, do you? Well let's test it and see. Look at all the items featured on this page for thirty seconds and then see how many you can remember and write down in one minute or less. There are fifteen items altogether.

PICTURE WORDS

Can you work out the hidden words
from the picture clues given on this page?

ANSWERS:

1. Accountant
2. Bagpipes
3. Poultry
4. Flyleaf
5. Crossroad
6. Hamster

51

FOR BETTER OR VERSE

There once was a restaurant in Crewe,
Where a man found a mouse in his stew,
Said the waiter, "Don't shout!
Or wave it about!
Or the rest will be wanting one, too."

A girl who weighed many an ounce,
Used language we could not pronounce,
When a fellow, unkind,
Pulled her chair out behind,
Just to see (so he said) if she'd bounce.

There once was a hunter called Sheppard,
Who was eaten for tea by a leopard.
Said the leopard, quite sad,
'You'd be tastier, lad,
If you had been salted and peppered."

There was a young lady called Perkins,
Who was terribly fond of fat gherkins,
One Sunday, at tea,
She ate nintey-three
And pickled her internal workings.

There was a young housewife from Gloucester,
Whose husband thought he had lost her.
To the freezer he bound,
When out came a sound,
The only problem now, to defrost her.

A mean old man of West Fentham,
Gnashed his false teeth, till he bent 'em.
When asked what the cost
of the teeth he had lost,
he said, "I don't know, I just rent 'em!"

There was an old lady of York
Who weighed much less than a cork.
She had to be fed
For six months on lead,
Before she could go for a walk.

A chicken from Timbuctoo
Confessed he was feeling quite blue,
"For," he said, "as a rule,
when the weather turns cool,
I'm likely to be in a stew."

THE LONG AND THE SHORT OF IT

Perhaps Birmingham should import a few gondolas, because it does have 22 more miles of canals than Venice.

The lead in an average pencil is sufficient to draw a line thirty five miles long.

There are approximately seventy three million books in the United States Library of Congress and 350 miles of shelving to hold them all.

Queanbeyan in Australia boasts a tandem for thirty one people.

During his lifetime, the average man will shave about thiry yards of whiskers off his face.

In 1976, an Englishman walked thirty six feet on stilts which were twenty two feet nine inches high.

When a baby kangaroo is born it is only one inch long.

King Charles I must have been one of the smallest kings in history. He was only four foot seven inches tall when fully grown.

Parliament Street is only twenty six inches wide, obviously not the place for chubby M.P.s.

During the French Revolution, there was a thirty-two-year-old midget, who carried out his spying activities dressed as a baby and was carried into enemy territory.

The shortest crossing between two continents is across the Bosphorus. It takes less than ten minutes to get from Europe into Asia.

The king cobra is so poisonous, that 150 people could be killed with just one gram of its venom.

ENTER, THE MAD SCIENTIST...

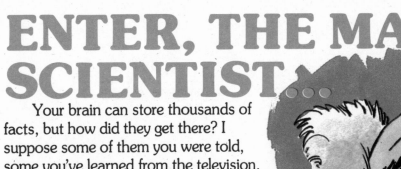

Your brain can store thousands of facts, but how did they get there? I suppose some of them you were told, some you've learned from the television, some you've read in books and some you've discovered yourself. If you like discovering things yourself, here are a few simple experiments for you to try, which all have something to do with the world around us. BUT REMEMBER, ASK AN ADULT IF IT'S O.K. BEFORE YOU TRY ANY OF THESE, OR BETTER STILL, ASK IF THEY WANT TO HELP YOU — AFTER ALL, THEY MIGHT LEARN SOMETHING TOO!

What Is It?

Heat 1 pint of milk in a saucepan (preferably an enamelled one) very slowly, until it is just slightly warm. You should be able to dip your finger into it quite comfortably, but do be careful! Take the pan off the heat and stir the milk as you slowly add half a glass of vinegar. You will see thick, white blobs beginning to form and if you keep on stirring they will eventually collect into a thick rubbery substance, from which you can squeeze the excess liquid, and take a closer look.

This is, in fact, **casein,** which is a special protein to be found in milk. Now we all know that protein is good for us, but did you know that this lump of particular protein is the basis for plastic? In the factory, the casein is extracted in a similar way, then it is dried, powdered and then mixed with a variety of colours, chemicals and water, depending on what the end result is to be.

So You Want to be a Spy?

Well, if you do, the first thing you will have to do is to learn how to send secret messages. Here's one method that you might like to try.

You will need a thick sheet of writing paper, some lemon juice and a pen with a clean nib. Write your message with the nib dipped in lemon juice, making sure that you have enough liquid on the nib to make clear writing. As it dries, it will disappear.

To read it again, you will need to put a lighted candle into the sink (this is the safest place to do this) and hold the sheet of paper about two inches above the flame, keeping it moving all the time, otherwise you'll set the paper on fire. It will only take a short time before you can read the message quite clearly.

If you want to experiment further, try using milk or grapefruit juice instead of lemon juice.

Now You See It, Now You Don't, Now You...

What happens to the sugar that you stir into your tea? Yes, you're quite right, it dissolves and you probably think that that's the end of it—but not necessarily.

Boil a glass of water in a saucepan and once it is boiling turn down the heat to low. Now, gradually begin adding sugar, stirring it all the time, until no more sugar will dissolve in it. Two or three cups should be enough. Then pour the mixture very carefully back into the glass (a heat resistant tumbler is best, please don't use one of your mum's best glasses!).

Now, you'll need a length of cotton string, a little longer than the height of the glass. Tie one end of this to a pencil and the other end to a small weight, a large button or a paperclip will do. Lower the string into the glass of sugar solution, resting the pencil across the top of the tumbler.

Leave it in a warm place for a few days and you will see the sugar crystals re-forming along the string. Don't be impatient though and try to cool the liquid too quickly or it won't work, you'll get much larger crystals if you allow the liquid to cool very slowly.

The sugar crystals re-form because as the liquid cools it cannot hold all the dissolved sugar.

GUZZLING GAMES

If you've ever wanted a go at one of those messy games that they play on Crackerjack, then here's your chance, but I should ask your mum first. She might want to protect the carpet and furniture with some plastic sheeting before you begin...

Drink Doggy, Drink...

To play this game you'll need a dice and shaker, a large bowl of orange juice and a shower cap! Everyone sits in a circle around the bowl, then they each have a turn at throwing the dice. The first person to throw a six has to put on the shower cap and begin lapping orange juice from the bowl, just like a dog. Meanwhile, the rest of the circle continues to throw the dice, until another person throws a six. This person then takes over at the bowl and so on...

Bobbing for Apples

This is a very simple game to play. You just need a large bowl of water and an apple for each of the people playing. Everyone has to kneel down around the bowl with their hands behind their backs. The object of the game is to try and catch your apple with your mouth — and it isn't as easy as it sounds!

56

Flour Mountain

This game needs a little preparation. you will need to fill a pudding basin with flour, packing it very tightly. Then turn it on to a flat plate, just as though you were building a sandcastle. Remove the basin and put a small unwrapped sweet carefully on top. Each person playing, then has to remove one spoonful of flour, **very carefully,** without moving the sweet. The first person to let the sweet fall has to put their hands behind their back and eat the sweet off the flour.

Chocolate Chewing

Here's a game that I'm sure everyone will like. You will need several blocks of chocolate, a plate, a knife and fork and a dice. Everybody who throws a six has a go at eating the chocolate which has been placed on the plate, with a knife and fork. They have to eat as much as they can before someone else throws a six and takes over. It's even funnier if they have to put on a bib before they can start eating!

TIDDLYWINKS OF THE YEAR SHOW

Here's a very simple game which can be made in minutes and will give you hours of fun.

You will need:

plasticine
some plastic drinking straws
tiddlywinks.

Now, simply make up some jumps, like the ones shown here, or you might like to design some of your own. Place them at varying distances apart and flick your tiddlywinks over them. You can play this game by yourself (enter three or four 'horses' if you like), or you can get together a number of friends and make a real competition of it.

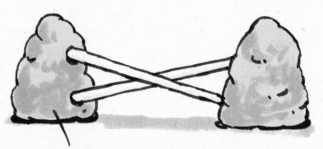

PLASTICENE

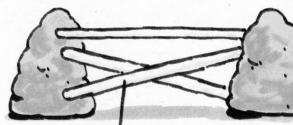

DRINKING STRAWS.

QUICK QUIZ

By answering all the questions on this page and re-arranging the first letter of each, you will find a hidden word.

1. I am a time of the year and a very merry

one, too.

2. I'm a farmyard animal and an alarm clock, too.

3. It's a description for Kings and also for blue.

4. You can always find me in Wonderland.

5. I'm the secret of the lock.

6. Without one your leg wouldn't bend.

7. I'm a vegetable, but they call me a flower.

8. I'm always good for a laugh.

9. The summer wouldn't be the same without me growing in the garden.

10. If you have one of me a day, I'm supposed to keep the doctor away.

11. You wouldn't believe that an animal as big as I am could be afraid of mice.

ANSWERS

1 Christmas **2** Cockerel **3** Royal **4** Alice **5** Key **6** Knee **7** Cauliflower **8** Joke **9** Rose **10** Apple **11** Elephant (the hidden word is **CRACKERJACK,** of course).

JUST A THOUGHT

What happened to the man who was given memory pills by the doctor—he forgot to take them!
A really good excuse is one which you can use over and over again!

The biggest strides towards road safety are made by those pedestrains with the longest legs!

It's sometimes a good idea to put off until tomorrow something that you should have done today—someone may have invented a machine for doing it by then!

When an optician makes a mistake—He makes a spectacle of himself!
Gargling is a very good way of finding out whether your neck leaks or not…

The reason that most children are so happy is that they don't have any children of their own to worry about!

61

HAVE YOU SEEN IT?

How observant are you? Well let's see. Here are some pictures of fairly familiar things, how many of them do you recognize?

7

8

9

10

11

12

HOW OBSERVANT ARE YOU?

At a glance these two pictures look identical. But look more closely and you'll see that isn't the case at all.

There are thirteen differences altogether, see if you can spot them all.

ANSWERS:

Picture B differs in the following ways:

1 an extra T.V. camera; **2** the monitor screen is on the left not the right; **3** the presenter has odd shoes; **4** there are only two microphones; **5** one camera hasn't any power line; **6** one camera man has on different trousers; **7** there are only six overhead lights; **8** one camera man hasn't any headphones; **9** the studio clock shows different times; **10** warning lights off; **11** the presenter hasn't a microphone on the camera; **12** no handles on the camera; **13** slightly different scenery;

I COULD CRUSH A GRAPE

How do you feel about crushing a few grapes? Well here's your chance.

You'll need to cut out some discs, like the ones shown here; thirty for each bunch of grapes. A shaker and a dice and another person to play with.

You choose which bunch of grapes you'd each like to have, purple or green. Each player has to throw a six to start, then the object of the game is to cover or crush every grape on the bunch with the discs.

E.g. If you throw a 5 with the dice. Cover up a grape with a corresponding number 5 on it.

You can only cover a number which you have thrown on the dice. Each person has to take it in turns to throw the dice.

The first person to cover all his grapes is the winner.

DISCS FOR ← COVERING GRAPES

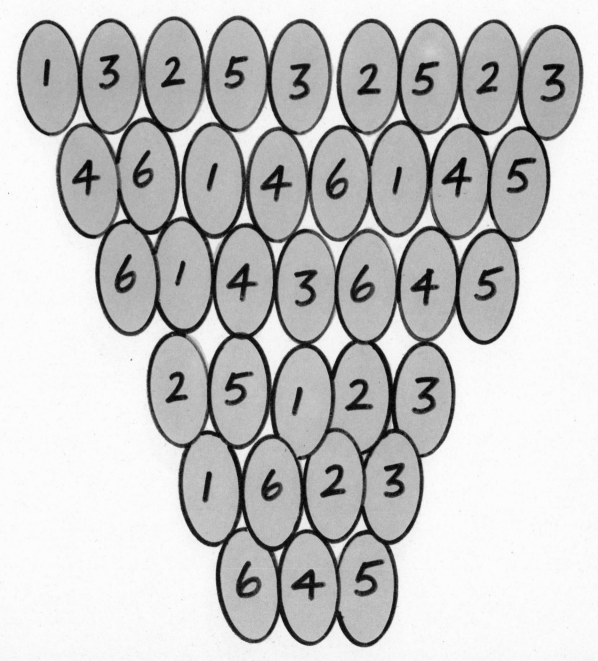

YOU HAVE GOT TO BE JOKING

Fed up of all those quizzes to which you don't know any of the answers? Well, never mind, here are a few more…but at least these **should** make you laugh!

Q: Why do bees always have sticky hair?
A: Because they have honey combs, of course!

Q: What do they call a man who inspects rabbit holes?
A: A Borough Surveyor.

Q: What uses a pen, but cannot write?
A: A pig.

Q: What kind of weather do rats and mice dislike the most?
A: When it's raining cats and dogs.

Q: Where do ducks keep their savings?
A: In the river bank.

Q: Who gets the most kicks out of his job?
A: A footballer.

Q: What is the most important part of a horse?
A: His mane (main).

IT'S A BIT FISHY

These fish may look very ordinary, but have you ever seen cardboard fish swim?

Sharks, piranha, goldfish, guppies, it doesn't really make a lot of difference what kind of fish they are, so long as you make them as they are shown here and so long as you have something to help them along.

Instructions

1. Cut out the fish or fishes (if you fancy a race) on thick card.
2. Cut a channel down the middle, finishing with a small circle, as shown.
3. Place the fish in a bowl of water, then add the magic ingredient. A little light oil, the sort that mum has for her sewing machine is the best. Put a couple of drops of this in the hole at the end of the channel and watch your fish go!

FOOTNOTE:

It's better to use a large bowl or tub, to stage the races and don't forget to change the water if it starts to get too oily.

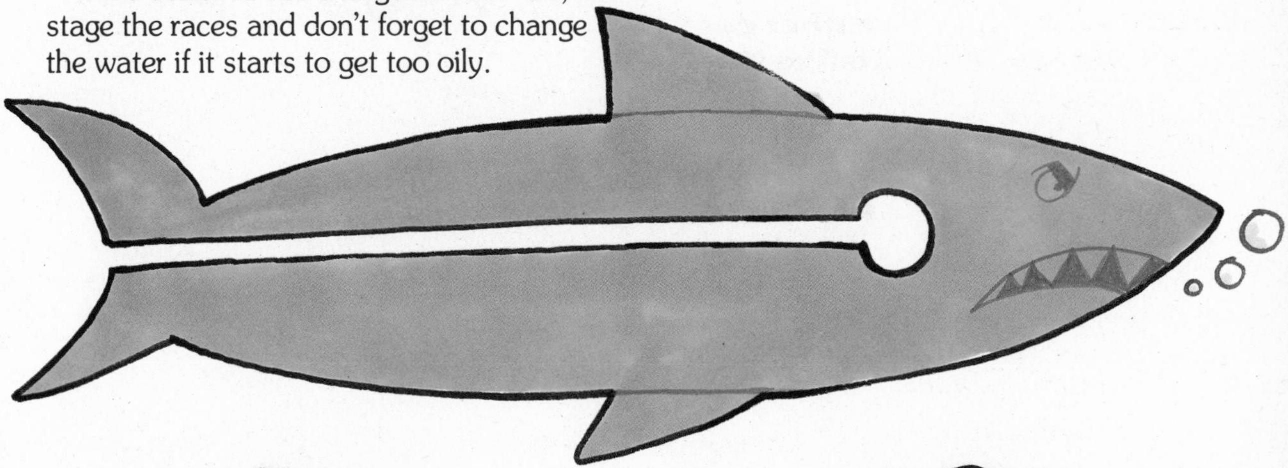

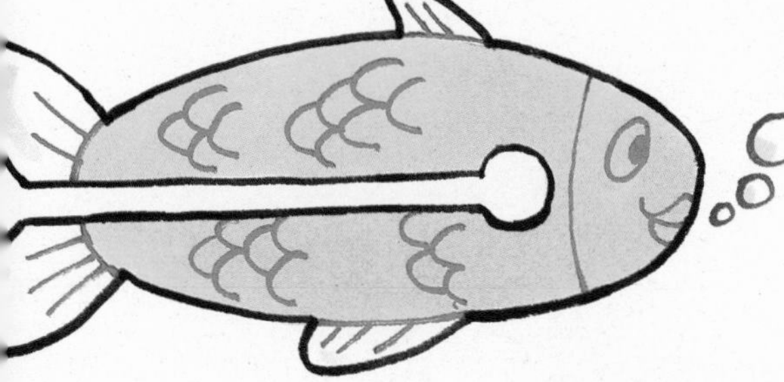

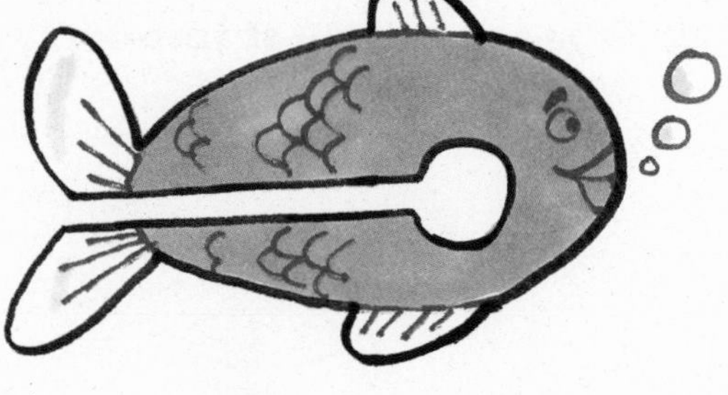

UNUSUAL UNIFORM

You may have noticed that Jimmy's school uniform is a little unusual in some respects. He's sent you a few tips, just in case you'd like to look as **fandabbidosy** as he does!

CAP – CROOKED

TIE – CROOKED, AND WITH THE REMAINS OF AT LEAST FOUR SCHOOL DINNERS CLEARLY VISIBLE

SHIRT – GRUBBY AND WITH SEVERAL BUTTONS MISSING

BLAZER – GRUBBY, ONE POCKET TORN AND THE REST BULGING WITH ALL SORTS OF THINGS

TROUSERS – KNEE-LENGTH AND BAGGY

SOCKS – WRINKLED AROUND THE ANKLES

SHOES – SCUFFED AND ONE SHOELACE UNDONE

WARNING: Parents and Teachers may not think this look is FANDABBIDOSY…

BACK TO NATURE

It's easy to forget in these scientific and technological times, the simple things in life, especially those in nature.

Here are two things to remind you. With one you can help nature and with the other, nature can help you.

Just for the Birds

This is a very simple bird feeder that you can make, to encourage the birds to come into your garden. It costs very little and it's very simple to make.

You'll need:

An empty cardboard fruit juice or milk carton.
Some sharp scissors.
Gloss paint (lead free).
A length of string.

All you have to do:

Cut out the four sides of the container, as shown. Paint the outside with gloss paint. When it's dry put a hole in the top to thread the string through and hang it up. Don't forget to put in some food regularly, especially in the winter. Crumbs, peanuts (NOT THE SALTED KIND), birdseed, bits of bacon rind will all be very tempting to the birds in your neighbourhood.

LET'S GET TOGETHER

The next time you're stuck indoors on a wet afternoon with a few friends and nothing to do, perhaps you could try some of these games, they're great fun.

Grandmother's footsteps

First of all you have to choose somebody to be Grandmother! 'She' then stands at one end of the room and everybody else stands at the opposite end. The object of the game is to creep up on 'her' without being caught. The person chosen to be 'Grandmother' may turn round at any time and anyone who she catches moving must return to the beginning and start again. The winner, of course is the first person to reach 'Grandmother'.

SSHHH!

Your mum will appreciate this game—the main objective is to keep as quiet as possible, until the final part at least. Everyone has to sit in a circle, one person then has to whisper a sentence into their neighbour's ear, this person then whispers it to the next, and so on. The last person has to say the sentence out loud, when everyone can compare it to the original—to which it often bears little resemblance!

Just Taste It!

You can have great fun with this, especially if you're in charge… You'll need to choose six different sorts of food; bread, jam or honey, a piece of apple, a bit of cake, some sugar, and if you're feeling a bit mean, a **tiny** bit of salt. Put the food out on different saucers and then each person has a taste, but they must be wearing a blindfold. You'll be quite surprised at some of the guesses you get…or try a little lemon juice, if you want to see some funny faces.

Charades

Here's a chance for all those budding actors and actresses to prove just how good they are. Take it in turns to act out a word or a well known phrase and the rest of the group have to guess what it is from your actions. You can either tell them at the begining how many words are involved and whether they're from a book or film or television etc., or you can act out this part of the mime, too.

SPOOKY SPOOFS

1st Ghost: Did you see me come in, just now?

2nd Ghost: Yes, of course.

1st Ghost: You've never seen me before though, have you?

2nd Ghost: No, I haven't.

1st Ghost: Then, how did you know it was me in the first place!

What do short-sighted spooks wear?

Spooktacles, of course!

Who saves drowning ghosts?

The Ghost Guard.

How do ghosts get through locked doors?

With their skeleton keys.

How do you ruin a ghost's bike?

Put a spook in his wheel.

What's the largest ghostly animal?

An elephantom.

Where do vampires meet in New York?

At the Vampire State Building.

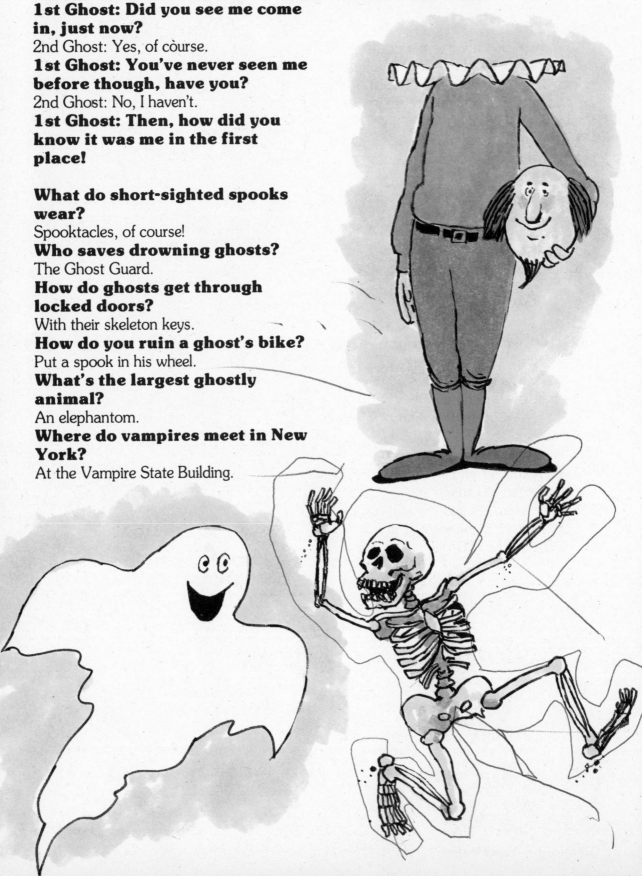

SPORTING CHANCE

Perhaps you are like Stu Francis and list all kinds of sports as your favourite hobby. If you do, you might like to try this quiz and see just how much you know about various sports.

1. This game originated in 1863 at the home of the Dukes of Beaufort. What is it?
2. 'Pot Black' is a well known term from which sport?
3. What would you be doing on the Cresta Run?
4. For which sport is Robin Cousins famous?
5. In which game would you use a 'puck'?
6. Tsu-chin was played in China in the third and fourth centuries B.C. It is still played in a similar way today, what is it called now?
7. Olga Korbut made a name for herself in which sport?
8. Which game began life as 'Baggataway' and was played by the American Indians?
9. Which famous sport would you be able to see if you were at the Indianapolis 500?

Odd Stu Out

Only two of these pictures of Stu are exactly the same. Do you know which?

A

B

C

D

E

ANSWERS PAGE

A A charm to cure hay fever; B Herbs; C Pea Crabs, their shells are approximately ¼″ in diameter; D King Charles spaniels, named after Charles II; E African; F Denmark, in 1219; G South Africa; H Sir Christopher Sydney Cockerell; I b; J The box jellyfish of the Pacific and Indian Oceans, they can kill a victim in less than 3 minutes; K I don't know; L Moths and Butterflies; M From the Latin, mille passuum, which means 1000 paces; N A lump, usually of gold or silver; O The Common Pacific Octopus; P Shrove Tuesday; Q Lady Jane Grey, she reigned for only nine days; T The American president, Theodore Roosevelt; U Russia; V Antofalla in Argentina; W 1509, by Peter Henlein of Nuremburg; X Foreigners; Y In the Phillipine jungles, they were used as a weapon; Z A high structure.

1 It's a royal residence in Scotland 2 Istanbul
3 People from Liverpool, Manchester and Glasgow
4a United States of America b New Zealand c Canada
d Australia 5 The Dead Sea, it has a high concentration of mineral salts 6 Egypt 7 Australia, Wales 8 Surtsey
9 Russia 10a France b Spain c England d Germany

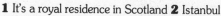

1. (d);
2. (a) four (b) eight (c) three
3. (a) Great Britain; (b) Italy; (c) Ireland
4. (a) Sycamore; (b) Horse Chestnut; (c) Holly; (d) Oak
5. (a) No Entry; (b) Two-way traffic straight ahead; (c) Opening or Swing Bridge; (d) Side road
6. (a) Pig; (b) Horse; (c) Elephant; (d) Frog; (e) Duck
7. (a) Humpty Dumpty; (b) Polly; (c) Little Jack Horner

1e; 2d; 3b; 4a; 5c.

1. Fungus, the most poisonous in the world.
2. Airships.
3. Newspaper.
4. Dogs.
5. Adam.
6. Beatles.
7. Insects.
8. Daley Thompson.
9. Oceans.
10. Solar.
11. Insurance.
12. FANDABIDOSI.

1. Giant Panda
2. Davy Crockett
3. Rainbow
4. Aladdin
5. Tree kangaroo
6. Phonograph, which was later to become the record player.
7. Ostrich
8. Dogs
9. Parsley
10. Human body

1. Sorry Stu. It sounds like a good idea, but by blowing on to the sails, they were moving backwards (like a rocket shoots forward into space when its jet of gas moves backwards on take-off). Stu and co., cancelled out any forwards motion. They all had very tired arms.
2. Yes, he was right. Hot water has slightly less density than cold, so that anything sinking through it would travel a little faster, including Stu!
3. Wrong again Stu! Because water molecules in a wave move up and down and not forwards, any floating item travels in a circular motion and is not carried along by the wave. Nearer the shore, however, where the water is shallower, the wave 'breaks', the water molecules surge forward and are able to push things in to the land.

1. Australia
2. Chrysanthemum
3. Post Office Tower
4. Shetland pony
5. Kingfisher
6. Tower Bridge
7. Television camera
8. Shark
9. Dragonfly
10. Puffin
11. St Paul's Cathedral
12. Saturn

1. Badminton
2. Snooker
3. Tobogganing
4. Ice skating
5. Ice hockey
6. Football
7. Gymnastics
8. Lacrosse
9. Motor racing
10. (a) cricket; (b) table tennis; (c) golf